Appropriating Truth

Abiding in the Revelation of Christ Through Faith's Embrace!

Rudi Louw

1

Table of Content

The Marvel of the Holy Bible

1. Uninterrupted Theme and Inspired Thought

It took *1,500 years* to compile the Holy Bible, involving *more than 40 different authors.* Yet the theme and inspired thought of Scripture continues *uninterrupted* from author to author, from beginning till end.

2. Absence of Mythical Stories

Compare philosophies and theories about creation in the Middle East, Europe, Asia, Africa, and Latin America and you'll find mythical scenarios: gods feuding and cutting up other gods to form the heavens and the earth, etc.

In ancient Greek mythology, the Greeks see Atlas carrying the earth on his shoulders. In India, Hindus believe eight elephants carry the earth on their backs.

But in contrast, Job, the oldest book in the Holy Bible, declares that, *"God suspends the earth on nothing."(Job 26:7)*

This was said millennia before Isaac Newton discovered the invisible laws of gravity that delicately balance every planet and sun in its individual circuit.

Contrary to every other ancient attempt to give a creation account, *the Holy Bible pictures the creation of the earth in a very scientific manner.*

For example, in Genesis Chapter One, the continents are lifted from the seas, then vegetation is formed and later animal life, all reproducing *'according to its own kind',* **thus recognizing the fixed genetic laws.** In addition, we have the bringing forth of man and woman, *all done by God in a dignified and proper manner, without mythological adornments.*

The balance or remainder of the Holy Bible follows suite.

The narratives are **true historical documents,** *faithfully reflecting society and culture* **as history and archaeology would discover them thousands of years later. Not only is the Holy Bible historically accurate, it is also reliable when it deals with scientifically provable subjects.**

It was never intended to be a textbook on history, science, mathematics, or medicine. *However, when its writers touch on these subjects,* **they often state facts that scientific advancement would not reveal, or**

6

even consider, until thousands of years later.

While many have doubted the accuracy of the Holy Bible, time and continued research have consistently demonstrated that the Word of God is better informed than its critics.

3. Intactness

Of all the ancient works of substantial size, *the Holy Bible survives intact, against all odds and expectations.*

Compared with other ancient writings, the Holy Bible has more manuscripts as evidence to support it than any ten pieces of classical literature combined!

The plays of William Shakespeare, for instance, were written about four hundred years ago, after the invention of the printing press. Many of his original writings and words have been lost in numerous sections, *yet the Holy Bible's uncanny preservation has weathered thousands of years of wars, contradictions, persecutions, fires and invasions.*

Through the centuries Jewish scribes have preserved the Holy Bible's Old Covenant text, ***such as no other manuscripts have ever been preserved. They kept tabs on every letter, syllable, word and paragraph.*** *They* *continued from generation to generation to appoint and train special groups of men within their culture* **whose sole duty it was to preserve and transmit these documents <u>with perfect accuracy and fidelity</u>.**

Who ever bothered to count the letters, syllables, or words of Plato, Aristotle, or Seneca for that matter?

When it comes to the New Testament, the actual number of preserved manuscripts is so great that it becomes overwhelming. *There are more than 5,680 Greek manuscripts, more than 10,000 Latin Vulgate manuscripts and at least 9,300 other versions. Further still, there exists an additional 25,000 manuscript copies of portions of the New Testament.* **No other document of antiquity even begins to approach such numbers.**

The closest in comparison is Homer's <u>Iliad</u>, with only 643 manuscripts. The first complete work of Homer only dates back to the 13th century.

4. Unmatched Accuracy in Predictive Foretelling

The Holy Bible is unmatched in accuracy in predictive foretelling. No other ancient work succeeds in this, or even begins to attempt it.

Other books such as the Koran, the Book of Mormon, and parts of the Veda claim divine inspiration; **but none of these books contain predictive foretelling.**

This one undeniable fact we know for certain: *While microscopic scrutiny would show up the imperfections, blemishes, and defects of any work of man, <u>it magnifies the beauties and perfection of God</u>. Just as every flower displays in accurate detail the reflection and perfection of beauty, <u>so does the Word of Truth when it is scrutinized</u>.*

Historian Philip Schaff wrote:

*"Without money and weapons, Jesus the Christ conquered more millions than Alexander, Caesar, Mohammad, and Napoleon. Without science and learning, He (Jesus the Christ) shed more light on things human and divine than all philosophers and scholars combined. Without the eloquence of schools, He (Jesus the Christ) spoke such words of life as was never spoken before or since and produced effects which lie beyond the reach of orator or poet. Without writing a single line, He (Jesus the Christ) set more pens in motion and furnished themes for more sermons, orations, discussions, learned volumes, works of art, and songs of praise **than the whole army of great men of ancient and modern times combined.**"* (*The Person of Christ*, p33. 1913)

Today, there are literally billions of Bibles in more than 2,000 languages.

Isn't it about time you find out what it really has to say?

Hey listen, the Holy Bible is all about Jesus, the Messiah, the Christ...

...and everything about Jesus Christ is really about YOU!!

Study Tips:

Read 2 Corinthians 5:14, 16, 18, 19, and 21.

In the light of these Scriptures, it should be obvious that, if you want to study the Holy Bible, *you should study it in the light of Mankind's redemption!*

Feed daily on **redemption realities** found in the book of Acts, in Romans Chapters One through Eight, and in Ephesians, Colossians, and Galatians. These realities may also be found in 1 Peter Chapter One, 2 Peter Chapter One, James Chapter 1, as well as in 1 and 2 Corinthians.

10

Acknowledgment

I want to acknowledge and thank one of my mentors in the faith, Francois du Toit, for blessing and impacting me with revelation knowledge.

I borrowed the portion on *"The Marvel of the Holy Bible"* from his website: http://www.MirrorWord.net as students so often feel they have a right to do with things that come from teachers they respect. Just as Galatians 6:6 says: *"Let him who is taught the Word **share in all good things** with him who teaches."*

To all our dear friends and family, for all the love and support, and to Chase Aderhold and all those who helped me with this project:

THANK YOU!

Especially to my wife, Carmen

For being my companion in life and partner in ministry and for keeping me real by being the one that sometimes has the unpleasant task of confronting me about appropriating God's truth in my own heart and life.

I love and appreciate you so very much!

Foreword

Thank you for taking the time to read this book.

Let me start off by saying that *I am totally addicted to my Daddy's love for me.*

I am in love with Jesus Christ, *and that is enough for me!*

The love of God is so much more than a doctrine, a philosophy, or a theory. It is so much more and goes so much deeper than knowledge: *it way surpasses knowledge.*

We are talking heart language here.

I write *to impact people's hearts,* to make them see the mysteries that have been hidden in Father God's heart concerning Christ Jesus, and really *concerning THEM.* I do this so as to arrest their conscience with it, *that I may introduce them to their original design and their true selves,* **presenting them to themselves perfect in Christ Jesus,** *and setting them apart unto Him* **in love,** as a chaste virgin.

We are involved with the biggest romance of the ages!

Therefore, this book cannot be read as you would a novel: *casually.* It is not a cleverly devised little myth or fable. **It contains**

13

revelation and *truth* about some things you may or may not have considered before.

It is the TRUTH of God, ultimate TRUTH, and therefore has direct bearing upon YOUR life. **The Word and the Spirit are my witness** *to the reality of these things!*

Be like the people of Berea who the Apostle Paul ministered to in Acts 17:11. Open yourself up to study the revelation contained in this book, *to* *to discover for yourself the reality of these things.*

Be forewarned, and do not become guilty of the sins of the Pharisees, **or you too will miss out on the depth of fulfillment God Himself, who is LOVE, wants to give <u>YOU</u>**.

Jesus said of the Pharisees and Sadducee that they strain out every little gnat BUT swallow whole camels. What He meant by that is that *some people seem to have it all together when it comes to doctrine and they love to argue.*

It makes them feel important but it is nothing other than EMPTY religious and intellectual pride.

*They know the Scriptures in and out and YET they are still so IGNORANT about **REAL TRUTH that is only found in LOVE.***

*They are still so ignorant and indifferent **towards the things that REALLY MATTER.***

14

They are always arguing over the use of *every little jot and tittle* and over the meaning and interpretation of *every word of Scripture.*

The exact thing they accuse everyone else of doing though, the precise thing they judge everyone else for, *they are actually doing themselves.* That is, **they often completely misinterpret and twist what is being said, *making a big deal of insignificant things, while obscuring or weakening God's real truth: the truth of His LOVE.***

They are always majoring on minors **<u>because they do not understand the heart of God</u>, and therefore they constantly miss the whole point of the message**.

Paul himself said it so beautifully:

*"...the letter kills but **the Spirit BRINGS LIFE**..."*

*"...<u>knowledge puffs up</u>, but **LOVE EDIFIES**..."*

I say again:

Allow yourself to get caught up in the revelation I am about to share.

Open yourself up to study the insight contained in this book, *not only with a desire to gain knowledge, but also with anticipation **to hear from Father God yourself, to encounter Him through His Word, and to embrace truth in*** *order to know and believe the LOVE God has for <u>you.</u>*

*Get so caught up in it **that you too may receive from Him LOVE'S impartation of LIFE.***

If you take heed to these things and yield yourself fully to it, **it is custom designed and guaranteed to forever alter and enrich your life!**

"Behold,
I am laying in Zion
a stone
that will make men stumble,
a rock
that will make them fall;"

"...and yet
he who believes in Him
will not
be put to shame."

- Romans 9:33

Prayer

It is our privilege and joy, Father, to know Your person and to encounter Your presence.

We thank you that we no longer stand far off, as spectators who are longing for a day that we would be brought nearer, but right now, we may already come with a new, bold confidence upon this new and living way which You Yourself have opened for us, through the torn veil; *the incarnate Word* …the Word that became more than prophecy, more than philosophy …the Word that became flesh and not only dwelt amongst us, *but was revealed to be within us!*

And we thank you that that flesh body was torn open **on our behalf**, and that everything that that flesh represented ***concerning the Fall and its influence upon us,*** faced the passion of the universe's only supreme Judge; the God who is a white-hot, all consuming, love-furnace!

Ha... ha... ha...

We thank You Daddy that You dealt it all a death blow in Jesus, ***on our behalf!***

We thank you, Jesus, that *you died in our stead* …**so that we would be translated from death into life!**

So that we might be made the righteousness of God in You; *in that one act of righteousness!*

Thank You that we have our original righteousness restored back unto us, in Christ Jesus, *in that successful work of redemption!*

Thank You, Father, that in His death, *we might be identified!*

And in His sonship *we may enjoy sonship!*

And so, Father, we know You today as our *"ABBA,"* as our **Daddy**, and we adore You for Your love that You have shed abroad in our hearts *and awakened there ...Your absolutely overwhelming, awesome love, which makes faith **a living reality within us!***

O we thank you Father that **faith works by this love!**

Father, we thank you *for each other,* we thank you that we may extend the love that You have shed abroad and awakened in our hearts, *that we may extend it to one another!*

And together we may all now be embraced in the household of God!

Father, we thank you that as we open the Scriptures, Your very own Spirit opens our understanding and that we perceive and behold wonderful things out of Your inspired words hidden in those writings of old.

We thank you that Jesus is glorified today in our fellowship together in this book.

Amen

Chapter 1

An End to All Disputes

In this book we are still focusing our attention on the theme of this **Faith Inspired Ministry** series which is to help people fully appreciate and appropriate the faith of God, i.e. that truth about us, *so clearly revealed in Jesus Christ, and in the gospel about His successful work of redemption.*

And if you haven't gotten the other books in this **Faith Inspired Ministry** series, *you should really get them and study them,* **because so much is being said and revealed that, *if you can fully grasp these things, you will continue to be blessed for years to come.***

So, just as a quick overview, in the previous book in this series we looked at and focused our attention upon *the practical appropriation of what legally belongs to us in this love-covenant which God made within Himself, between Himself and His original blueprint Son, Jesus.*

We are His offspring, and benefactors of this covenant. *We are benefactors of what legally belongs to us **in this love-covenant!***

Isn't it so wonderful to discover that the Bible contains more than mere religious information!

Ha... ha... ha...

It truly is just mind-blowing when you begin to discover that there is more to this Book, the Bible, than just an old time history of some Middle Eastern nations that most of us cannot even relate to! And let me tell you it is also so much more than just a recorded history of some great men who supposedly knew God, in ancient times.

Listen, the day that you discover that this Book, the Bible, **is but a mere reference <u>to a legal contract</u>** *that existed in the heart of God for all eternity **concerning <u>you</u>** is the day your whole world changes!*

Ha... ha... ha...

Hallelujah!

In this Book, the Bible, *in that covenant, in that legal contract **referred to** in the Old Covenant portion, **and fully revealed and talked about** in the New Testament,* God expressed in vocabulary, in language, ***His heart!***

He defined there *the dream of His heart **towards the human race; towards <u>us</u>!***

Listen, God has given such accurate definition of and to His heart dream, in this Book, the Bible, that He has articulately employed, every

24

intellectual means necessary *whereby Man could* **successfully comprehend and communicate the Father's very own integrity and intention.**

And thus, by employing Man's intelligence and communication skills, by employing language, God employed every means necessary *by which Mankind could* **grasp His faithfulness.**

These things can be fully known; **it is expanded upon in the Scriptures, in the Holy Bible,** *especially so in its New Testament portion.*

The reason for the Bible, and the very reason for the incarnation of Jesus Christ, *is because of God's desire not to be misunderstood.*

God Himself even entered into an oath, as if He, of all beings, could not be trusted.

You see, if two people decide on some kind of business venture together, they might get very excited about the prospects and the possibility of joining forces and combining their financial resources, and maybe some other resources also, you know: their stuff.

So they would get very excited over the idea of combining their minds and their thoughts and their plans and their dreams. But you see, *there would always remain the risk that one of the two could not be trusted.* And so a higher and greater authority would be employed to

25

add **greater integrity** and **greater weight** *to the purity of their intention.*

This is what gave birth to the practice in business and even in marriage, that people indeed swear by one higher and greater than themselves, such as a lawyer backed by a judge, and a very powerful governmental system, *in order to* **put an end to all possible dispute**, *in the now, or in the future,* and thus, they employ every possible means whereby they could *add to their* **sense of security.** They would add, therefore, the oath, to bolster their sincerity, *because they desire not to be misunderstood.* And so, at the same time, they also make room, for the possibility that their friend could not perhaps be trusted, and thus they employ a higher and greater authority which they both swear by. And so in this oath, **all disputes are put to an end.**

In the Afrikaans translation it puts it so beautifully. It carries the idea of *putting to an end* **all back and forth bickering.** *By employing an oath, people are putting to an end* **any possible <u>contrary</u> argument.** *It is the end of* **all <u>disagreement</u>; the end of <u>all</u> argument; the full stop – the <u>final point</u> beyond which one cannot go!**

So, no matter what could ever happen in the future, to contradict their intention; *their original contract,* <u>**it is as good as taken care of already through the oath**</u>.

Thus the original contract is reinforced and enforced!

Just so, in God's heart dream, *He has given Himself wholeheartedly and completely to Mankind **in covenant integrity!***

God did not just give Himself to us in some kind of reluctant religious way, or in just some kind of inferior, meaningless, religious philosophy!

No. He gave Himself to us, He gave His heart to us; His commitment, *in covenant integrity!*

As if He could not be trusted.

This is so amazing I have to say it again so it can sink in: **He gave Himself to us, His devotion, His care, His whole heart, His everything, *in covenant commitment, in covenant integrity!***

And so, as opposed to the Old Hebrew Covenant which was between God and Man, *in the New Covenant we discover that the second party is now God Himself.* He swore by Himself, by His own being, *incarnate* in a human body!

Being our original blueprint and now also one with the human race in the incarnation, *this Jesus forever became our inseparable representative.*

(In order to better understand this, you need to get my books entitled: *"God's Eternal Purpose", "God's Love for You!"* and *"God's Inheritance in You!" also perhaps, "Offspring of God." and then also the Study Course, "The Gospel in 3-D!"*)

Deity took upon Himself humanity *to become our inseparable surety.*

He became the surety of our eternal union with God!

He came and revealed that eternal union, and thus He also then re-established that union; *that oneness.*

Jesus, through the incarnation, and then the resurrection, became *the security of our union with God* <u>for all eternity</u>.

Isn't that wonderful?!

And so, it's in this understanding of God's own love-initiative, it is in the understanding of such an awesome act of love for us, by God Himself, that we approach the Scriptures in our study in this book.

Chapter 2

God's Initiative

When we approach the Scriptures, God wants us to understand the heart dream of the Eternal One; *of the eternal, ageless God!*

It is this God who invented and brought forth out of Himself a being **as His companion,** and then placed that being *in a body* which He Himself created and caused *to dwell on this beautiful planet* which was also created by Him.

Listen, in light of this; in the light of Man's true identity, in the light of Man being more than flesh and blood, *in the light of Man being brought forth out of God* **to be His companion and His image and likeness**, we have to approach the Scriptures *with a new mentality.*

As we study in the Scriptures, that Word, the *'LOGOS'* made flesh, **we begin to discover that God has given Himself to humanity _in absolute covenant integrity, in an oath,_ so that He cannot be misunderstood; so that *His intentions with us* cannot be misinterpreted.**

Hebrews 6:18 says that, *"...**this makes it impossible for God to be proved false**."*

*"…so that we, who have fled (to these truths and to Him) for refuge, **might have unwavering confidence!**"*

Hallelujah!

You see, in the light of these things, in the light of God's covenant integrity from His heart towards us, backed by an eternal oath, **our confidence is not based or built upon our initiative, but it is based and built upon His initiative!**

Praise God!

Thank you Father!

As we meditate upon His initiative; *that very initiative which He expressed from His heart **in loving us** ...**and loving us first** ...while we were still at enmity towards Him ...**while we were still in self-destruct mode, so hostile, and in such rebellion in our thinking towards Him** ...**and towards our whole design as His offspring; as His companions, brought forth in His image and likeness to fully represent Him** ...**even while being in that frame of mind, and in our hostile indifferent attitude towards Him, He still took the initiative <u>in His love for us</u>, in the incarnation and work of redemption** ...**just like He first took the initial initiative <u>in His love</u> when He created Man, way back in the beginning, in the garden.***

In His love, He took the initiative towards us, in Christ, **from His heart.**

He loved us first!

And as we think upon and ponder, and muse, and meditate <u>upon that truth</u>, *we begin to fall deeply in love with Him!*

...And so, in that environment our hearts are sealed to become immune to condemnation!

Hallelujah!

When we discover these things for ourselves, this settled secure covenant commitment of God; this love-covenant He made with us from His heart, ***becomes of such value and worth.*** It becomes such a weightiness within our hearts, such glory within our spirits, that *no contradiction can ever challenge it again!*

No contradiction can ever challenge again what God has secured in His Word, in His "LOGOS" made flesh!

That is precious news; priceless beyond compare!

We can only study and genuinely embrace and appropriate what God has made available for us and to us in promise and in covenant, *in the light of understanding the difference between two opposing principles.*

The one principle is called; **works,** which clearly suggests **Man's own efforts to obtain**.

And the other is called; **faith,** which clearly suggests **God's initiative and His undertaking <u>from the heart</u> on our behalf** to release us into a faith appreciation and application of that which we both understand in the Scriptures, and comprehend in His Word, the *"LOGOS"* made flesh.

If this might seem like heavy language that goes over your head, *I challenge you to pay close attention* and to just hang in there with me. *All of this will become clear as I go along.* And pretty soon you too will find out for yourself, that as you begin to try and express the volume of His working within you, language becomes too small to contain all the glory and magnitude of that truth and the enormous size of that love. After all, these are **eternal** *things* we are talking about …Just try and measure or contain that!

Ha… ha… ha…

No really, I often find that words become too small. There is not enough descriptive meaning in them and they become inadequate to try and express the working of a God who is love personified, and who deals with us in our inner-man, *and seeks to unveil Himself to us.*

And so quite often we begin to search for words, we begin to search for language. We go and we begin to dig into the original language just to try and discover the length, the breath, the height, the depth; *the awesome largeness of His love in His expression of Himself to us.*

And do you know what we discover to be so wonderful?

Even though language might increase in vocabulary, the explanation, the very revelation of His love, *remains as simple as it needs to be for even a child to comprehend it.*

Truly His teaching distills even upon the tender grass like the dew.

So I want you to just keep reading and listen with your heart as you do. Don't allow your mind to become distracted. If you read, maybe, an English word that you've never bothered to discover before, let alone think about the depth of its meaning, just keep reading and allow His teaching in this book to distill upon your heart as the dew. Let Him refresh you with His love, and quicken you in your spirit, and minister to you the life-breath of His Word, of His message, as you read.

Now where was I before I got raptured and carried away to heaven somewhere by that thought? Ha... ha... ha... Oh yes. Now I remember. We are saying to you, me and the Holy Spirit now, ha… ha… ha… that in our search, meaning yours and mine, *to effectively appropriate what now legally and practically belongs to us, we have discovered that it,* **indeed** <u>*legally*</u> **belongs to us**, *amen.*

We have discovered that this thick, big Book, the Bible, **contains the mere reference to a sacred contract** between the Creator of the entire universe, and this being that came forth out of Him, called Man, ***because of our eternal association with Christ!***

Our lives are hidden with Christ in God, amen!

We are co-heirs with Christ!

We are heirs of God!

Legal heirs, amen, ***not illegitimate heirs, but*** <u>***legal heirs,***</u> *amen!*

We are all wrapped up together, with Christ, in the bosom of our Father!

And so we not only have a reference to it, written down in Scripture, and accurately displayed in Jesus, *but we have the fine print in the contract:* ***God's very own design impressed within our own being;*** **it's been impressed within our very being!**

We have that fine print within the contract *expressed to us, clear as day,* ***in the person of Jesus Christ.***

O yes, we have **God's design** expressed to us ***in covenant language, in a legal***

34

unchanging contract, in an eternal oath, and in an eternal person.

And now in discovering and seeing these things our desire is to so appropriate these truths, these realities for ourselves in a faith-appropriation, *and to also help you appropriate these things in your understanding, and in your own faith, so that it does not leave any of us lacking in our lives, or still frustrated and imprisoned in an effort of our own: An effort which quite frankly does not match the standard of* **what is revealed** *in the New Testament Scriptures and in His Word; in Jesus,* **and is revealed to be in us already!**

So, having said all that, let us get focused now and study the appropriation **of** faith, or **what faith lays a hold of.**

Paul calls it, in Romans 1:5,

"…the obedience **of** *faith,"* speaking of the fruit of faith.

You see, **our faith** *is* **our obedience**.

That obedience to **believe what is being said** begins to bear fruit in our lives. *Faith produces its own fruit, amen!*

And what does our faith consist of? I mean, what is faith anyway? **Hey, faith is not complicated; faith simply means to SEE what God is saying and thus to agree with Him!**

35

It simply means, to SEE; *to comprehend, to grasp, to understand ...and thus to yield and agree!*

To have faith is to simply SEE or grasp *who God really is, according to His own revelation of Himself, **in the incarnation; in Christ Jesus!***

To have faith is to SEE and perceive and understand, not only who God has revealed Himself to be, **but also, *who He has revealed us to be,* *there in the incarnation; in Christ Jesus!***

Thus, faith is to know and comprehend and understand and therefore to believe that **God is love** and that **God loves me,** and that *I am not just a mere man;* I am a child of God – **I come from above;** I did not just originate in my mother's womb! **God is my true origin; *my Daddy!***

Thus, faith is **to SEE all that God has given me; all that belongs to me, and all that is already within me, *and to embrace it fully!***

If you haven't perhaps read *"Faith Inspired Obedience!"* and *"God's Unfailing Integrity"* yet, I want to encourage you to get it and read it.

It will help lay a foundation from which to build upon in your study of what is being said in this book and in the remaining books in this series.

Chapter 3

Discovering Him as Our Alpha

In discovering Scripture, **we are discovering Him!** We are discovering Him **as our Alpha** *...and* **as our Omega***, amen!*

He who began a good work within us; in our creation, and now within our understanding, within our faith, within our hearts, He is not going to give up on us half way and say, *"All right, I have given you a good start. Now you finish it!"*

It reminds me of this joke I heard once about this little boy who got an apple for lunch *but he had no front teeth.*

Being determined to eat the apple still, he went to the teacher and politely asked with a lisp, *"Excuse me sir, can you please give me a kick-ssthtart on this apple?"*

Ha... ha... ha...

Well let me assure you, God has more than a kick-ssthtart in mind for you, amen!

The good news is that the God who invented us and gave birth to us, and initiated our experience with Him, is the

same God who stands with you in covenant commitment, to complete your experience of Him, amen.

God *has fully equipped us* **to** <u>partake</u> **of everything He has desired for us in the beginning** *and now restored to us again,* **as a gift, in Christ Jesus!** *And He will personally bring us into the full understanding and experience of these things.*

He, the author of truth, the author of reality, stands ready *to establish* a new and greater reality for us!

He stands ready to *establish us* in His very own reality!

Isn't it wonderful to discover that we need not live any longer with the anxiety of *having begun in the Spirit, but now having to complete this whole thing in the flesh, in ourselves?!*

You see, your own efforts will always keep you limited to yourself, *but faith in His effort, faith in His achievement,* **releases you into the experience of His abundance and limitlessness in your spirit and life!**

Hallelujah!

Let's start in 1 Corinthians 15:56,

"The sting of death is Sin..."

In looking at the word *"death,"* we need to see it defined as everything that robs us of closeness, and creates a sense of separation in our relationship with God; *but it is nothing but an illusion; a lie.*

"Death" does not mean the extinguishing of Man. *You cannot be extinguished!* You are a spirit being! *You are an eternal being with an eternal destiny!*

The word *"death"* merely speaks of a separation.

And so Paul speaks of this here in 1 Corinthians 15:56 and he says that,

"The sting of death is Sin..."

"The sting..."

In other words, *the thing that **causes** death:*

*"The thing that **causes** death, is **Sin**..."*

*"...and the **power of Sin** is **the Law**."*

You see the Law of Moses comes and it reveals to Man *the power* of his problem.

Because if Sin were **a mere matter** of wrong thinking and wrong decision, *then Man could simply correct it through right thinking and right decision.* But the Law was given to Man, to reveal to Man, that Sin, and its fruit of sin, is a greater problem *than **mere** wrong conduct.*

39

You see, sin's problem is rooted in **a wrong mindset** *that expresses itself* – it is the very thing that drives that sin and wrong conduct, thus it expresses itself as a wrong nature.

And so, if God is going to have any lasting impact upon us, **if His redemption is going to have any lasting impact upon the human race,** *then He is going to have to deal with more than just* the cobwebs in life; **the cobwebs, the <u>surface</u> issues of sin and wrong conduct.** You see, if His redemption is going to have a lasting impact, *He has to deal with the spider of Sin <u>first</u>, He has to deal with that* **wrong mindset and belief-system of Sin, which we inherited in the fall, and which is at the <u>root</u> of all sin and misconduct!**

His redemptive work in your life therefore, *must deal with more than just* **the symptoms.**

He must deal with that **wrong mindset,** *which manifests as* **a wrong nature** *and produces* **sin and wrong conduct!** He must deal with that **<u>identity crises</u>; *that outright lie and deception we inherited in the Fall.*** It's like a virus or some sort of parasite, some outside force that has come in and laid a hold of you *and* **manipulates you** *and its nature finds* **expression** *in your person and in your* conduct! You see, God's redemptive work must not just *be able to,* **but must actually thoroughly deal** with that very **mentality, that very mind-set** and resulting manipulation of your person and your nature, giving birth to the symptoms of sin and wrong conduct.

Now if you study these things in the New Testament, you will find that the Law became the measure of Sin; *the measure of Sin's strength.*

We see in Romans Chapter Three how the full spectrum, the full reality of Sin, its total influence and power, its full consequences, *were displayed and portrayed in Man's* **inadequacy to consistently perform up to standard.**

Even though his conduct could be considered blameless in the eyes of the Pharisees, he could not remove the deception he had to hide behind in his own heart, when his own eyes would continue to cause him to stumble.

I mean this very faculty called *sight* that was designed by the Creator, became a member in his body that embarrassed him in his personal life.

This was the reality Paul himself **once** lived in. He says so in Romans Chapter Seven.

But as we begin to study and discover in the revelation given to us later by that same Paul, we clearly see that **after he received his spiritual sight he was set free himself.**

As we study these things, we discover in that revelation of the Word of the New Covenant, that **God has so dealt with Sin**, that **its nature, its dominion, its power over the human life, over the human mind and consciousness has been broken.**

But I am not going to get into all that right now. If you want, you can make a thorough study of it in my books *"Resurrection Life Now!"*, *"No Longer Looking for Applause!"* *"God's Measure Versus Man's Measure"*, *"Reigning in Righteousness"*, and also *"Zoë,"* as well as my Study Course or Book Series called, *"The Gospel In 3-D!"*

Now how do we tap in and enter into **the liberty and the freedom** that this covenant brings and introduces to us?

Paul defines his whole ministry in Romans 1:5 as, *"...bringing about the obedience of faith."*

There really are only two kinds of obedience.

The Law would enforce obedience **through reward and punishment**, which means that I will get you to change your behavior, I will get you to change your conduct; it doesn't matter if you're an elephant, a monkey, or a human being; I will eventually succeed in so changing your conduct and behavior *through the law of reward or punishment* that I get you to comply and do exactly what I want you to. I mean, how else are you going to get that parrot to talk or that elephant to perform funny tricks for you?

You see, the problem remains that even though your parrot can say, *"Praise the Lord, hallelujah!"* It is still going to remain a parrot!

The law of reward and punishment cannot affect that little creature's nature.

Oh, **it could change its conduct**… and you can change your parrot into a very religious, devout looking and appearing parrot. *But no amount of reward or punishment could ever successfully change the nature of that creature!*

And so the law served only to reveal **the nature of Man's condition,** *so that a new anticipation could be born in the heart of Man:* ***the anticipation of again being restored to original innocence;*** the anticipation of being able to live a life of enjoying innocence, beyond the frustrating limits of yesterday's effort.

I could successfully achieve my highest dream as a sportsman today *and then just as successfully spoil it again tomorrow.* **Revealing that there is no consistency in my own effort and my own ability.** There's no permanent consistency in my own excellence or skill.

And so God's faith comes, in the gospel, in Jesus, in the incarnation, and work of redemption, and replaces all that, and that faith of God concerning my true identity now restored, becomes my fuel. *It now*

energizes me with a new ability, which I am tapping into, through hearing with faith.

In Galatians Chapter Three Paul talks about, *"He who works mightily within you…"*

How does He do it?

How does the power of God work?

How do I get the things of God to work on my behalf?

Paul continues there and he asks,

"Does He do it, I mean, do these things work through the hearing of the Law, through the works of the law, through my own religious diligence that will eventually so twist God's arm that God cannot but bless me?"

"…or does it work through hearing with faith?"

Paul states,

*"…**it works through hearing with faith!**"*

He says,

*"…**in the same way** as Abraham's faith was reckoned to him as righteousness, **our faith is reckoned to us as righteousness!**"*

You see, **righteousness can only be <u>discovered,</u>** *through hearing with faith;* **not earned!**

Abraham merely <u>discovered</u> the approval of the Creator, *through faith in His word.*

You see, the motivation under the Law is confined to punishment or reward, *and therefore the best it could do is produce an inferior short-lived self-righteousness, because it's a motivation that is ruled by a consciousness of lack,* **but faith is the opposite of a consciousness of lack.**

While my life, my conduct, my dream in life is motivated by the Law, *I will be ruled by a consciousness of lack.*

And what does that produce?

Man's biggest enemy …it's called **guilt!**

And **guilt will imprison me to a sense of inferiority, to a sense of permanent inadequacy,** *and then cause me to have to achieve beyond yesterday,* to have to so impress someone, even if it is only my mother, but at least some positive applause will continue to feed my hunger for applause, because as I have said before, *we have been designed for applause.*

Listen, God did not have another hippo, or lion, or monkey, or pet in mind when He made you!

God had in mind, in Man, in YOU, a being that would reflect His own brilliance! He had in mind a being that He would not feel embarrassed about or ashamed of, *but a* *being of praise and applause and beauty; a being reflecting His very own righteousness.*

But Sin marred that reflection of the image of the Creator in Man, *and so Man was left in a void of seeking to again restore to himself what he lost.*

And in his effort, in his desperate longing for applause and recognition, he became a master at being a phony and a hypocrite. Having to so perform, so impress, that he eventually created a standard of so called *"wisdom,"* a false standard of righteousness that God had to come and expose for its own corruption.

That standard is called *worldly wisdom* and *noble birth.*

And the world would say, *"Tell me something about this person."*

And so we get these forms, you know, especially if you want to attend an institution of learning, a so called: *'higher institute of learning,'* like a university or even a Bible School or Seminary …and so you get these forms, and we have to have at least three close references or more, and they now have to fill out and answer questions like: *'Is this person an alcohol user, cigarette smoker …were they involved in a divorce? In your own words, tell us about this person; we'd like to know more about their past.*

Why?

Because, you see, *we now have to formulate an opinion about this person ...***based upon someone else's opinion of this person's past!***

That's exactly why God had to come in Christ and expose the corruption of worldly standards, that system of false righteousness, by literally taking the despised and rejected, those of low esteem, those of no esteem, the so called, nobodies, *and elevating them in the redemptive work of Jesus.*

And in Christ Jesus He restored us all to Himself, and to our original righteousness, our original identity and design as children of God, *so that there remains no basis for any confidence in the flesh!*

Paul says, *"What becomes of our boasting?"*

"...it's excluded!"

Oh, what a disappointment, Paul, after we worked so hard and put so much effort into it, you're saying, it no longer counts, it is excluded?!

Yes brother, yes my precious sister, you've got it!

Whether you're the biggest muscle-man in town, or the smartest, most intelligent brain-box on campus; whether you're the wealthiest financial guru in the city, or the most gorgeous girl in line for the next Miss America, or Miss

World title, or major modeling opportunity, **God is not impressed!**

God has never been impressed with all that as some surrogate righteousness that could possible replace your original righteousness! God is not impressed with your self-made righteousness, *because He sees a potential reflection in you,* **that can only be measured by His original design of you.**

Listen, God has greater confidence in His design of you, than in the so called strength or weakness of your flesh, or of your past, ruled by a wrong mindset manifesting as a supposed sinful nature.

God has greater confidence in the legal integrity, the legal reality of His eternal purpose, to restore you to righteousness, *than the effects of any temporal interruption to His design!*

A motivation ruled by the Law, *is a motivation ruled by* **a consciousness of lack,** always conscious of, *'I'm not there yet;'* of *'I am not, therefore I have to become!'*

'There may be some golden daybreak when I might get there, but right now brother, wow, if you guys only knew all that I am dealing with!'

And so this sin-consciousness; (the fruit of the wrong tree we partook of in the garden, and still partake of), that sin-consciousness captures me, *and captivates my full attention,*
48

and binds me up, and so now I have to continue to impress and perform, both in my fellowship with the brethren, and in my devotional life, and *basically in everything else I do in life.*

I have to continually try and seek some kind of response from Deity, *because I constantly remain unsure of myself.*

BUT Paul speaks of a new force, *which releases a new kind of energy in Man.*

Chapter 4

A New Force at Work in Us

In Colossians Chapter One, there in the last few verses, Paul talks of an energy that is mightily inspired within him. **It is an energy which takes him beyond disappointment,** even though in ministry he might sometimes be confronted with a very critical, negative attitude, in his fellow Man, or with another disappointing experience. BUT, he says, *there is an infusion of spirit-energy, an unhindered inspiration,* **that far exceeds all that.**

And so he says, *"**My ambition is to <u>present</u> every individual <u>already complete in Christ</u>, standing in the full excellence of His workmanship, and by that <u>revelation</u> to bring them to maturity in Him.**"*

This is why I believe that it is of the utmost importance for us to study and discover this truth of **faith-inspired obedience – *the obedience of faith.***

We must discover faith: **the faith of God revealed in the gospel.** *It must become our faith.* It is the only way to fully appropriate the truth which the Word, the gospel made flesh in Jesus, has revealed, and which is recorded there in the Scriptures, and therefore still available for us to discover.

In one of Paul's letters, he commends the people for their good testimony. But he says to them that, *"I want you to go beyond having a good testimony only when I am present with you."*

"I want you to have and hold that good testimony, not only when I am with you, but much more even when I am absent from you."

*"Much more when I am absent, I desire to see, and to hear about **a consistency in your life and faith**."*

He says, *"We are no longer involved in hypocrisy or in eye service, we are no longer Man-pleasers, we are no longer trying to perform before one another to see who can look the most mature, or the most intellectual with the most common sense, or the most Pentecostal, or the most spiritual, or the most pious, or the most religious.*

*Hey no! Listen brethren, we have discovered a standing in Him, in His approval of us, that liberates us t**o become the mirror** ...to **exhibit** the exact image of our Maker, of our Father, of our Daddy God, who is love ...**to simply be the expressed image** of His Divine nature!"*

Jesus said in Matthew 5:19 and 20 that,

*"Unless your righteousness **exceeds** the righteousness of the Pharisees, you've got a problem."*

The obedience of faith does not mean that God has now simply just lowered the standard that the Law presents *in order to accommodate our fallen state.*

No. The obedience of faith means that instead of relaxing even the least of the Law, *we now **fulfill it** by living out **our true original identity** to the fullest extent that it could possibly be **lived and fulfilled.***

...And we're able to do this because, you see, *we tap into a power that takes us far beyond our own **weak efforts in the flesh** to keep and uphold some **external** Law.*

Let me tell you something: The alpha, the very beginning of God's working within us, *ignites and begins to happen* when **we have our first encounter with the word of faith, *the gospel of our salvation.***

In the faith of God revealed, in the truth of God revealed in the gospel, we tap into a reservoir, an inexhaustible resource of Divine inspiration, *which now mightily energizes us from within.*

You see; the Law was but a shadow, pointing to something greater, to a greater reality, to the fact that the image and likeness of God, (the very Divine nature of God), is inscribed upon our inner-consciousness, *because it is already engraved upon our inner-man; **it's the very identity of our spirit.***

In the beginning of 1 Thessalonians Chapter One, Paul refers to that initial encounter with God in the word of truth, (in the gospel), and then to *the ever increasing impact* of the testimony of the saints, because of that encounter with God, *spreading beyond their region, reaching even to the uttermost parts of the earth!*

And then he shows us the secret of how that could possibly happen. He says there in 1 Thessalonians 2:13,

*"...and we also thank God constantly for this; that when you first **received the impartation of the truth** of the Word of God* (the truth of the gospel) *which you heard from us, **you embraced it,** not as the word of men, but instead, you **welcomed it;** you **received** it and **accepted it as reality; (as the truth** ...you accepted it for what it really is in truth), **the very Word of God Himself,** which now also mightily works within those who believe it!"*

Those two words *"**received**"* and *"**accepted**"* used in this verse are two different words in the Greek.

The one is the word, *LAMBANO* which means, **to catch, to lay a hold of, to seize an opportunity,** also, **to assume, to make a right or successful assumption, to perceive,**
54

thus, **to give full reception to, to conceive, to put on, to take as a man who takes a wife to himself.**

And then the word, DEGOMI is the second word used there, which means, **to take into one's hands, or to take into one's home or into one's heart, to receive into, to retain, to contain, to acquire a deep accurate knowledge of, to grant access to, to receive kindly, to welcome, to receive in hospitality, to entertain, to bear patiently with, to approve, to embrace, to agree fully with.**

So Paul uses these two beautiful big Greek words to say, *"Listen you guys, you know what, there is **a beginning** to everything in your lives, and if you want that thing to continue, **simply engage afresh with that very thing on a consistent bases.** In other words, stick to that which was the 'alpha;' **the initial thing that introduced that experience to you."**

*"What was the 'alpha' of your experience in the faith? **You heard a word** which we brought to you, and you know what you did with it? You took it beyond its natural value. You received it beyond its philosophical value, even beyond its religious, doctrinal, or theological value. **You received it and embraced it for what it really is: The truth; the very Word of God Himself!"** And the King James adds that,*

*"God, through that Word, is the very thing **which now mightily works within you!"***

What is it that is in that Word? What is invested in that Word **which now mightily works within us?**

The omnipotence of God, *the supernatural; the very power of God Himself is what is invested in that Word!*

Listen, God has exalted His Word above His name! He has placed His Word, **His gospel,** in a place of authority even above His name, *to confirm His name; to confirm His love!*

Hallelujah!

You see if He is JEHOVAH SHALOM, **the God of tranquility, *the God that releases my mind from anxiety* ...*then His truth, His Word guarantees my escape!***

His Word guarantees the effect, which that liberty that it produces within you, brings to you!

He has truly exalted His Word **above** His name.

Paul says, *"I thank God that as you heard the word which we brought to you, you embraced it. You did all these wonderful things that we just looked at with that Word, and **it is now mightily at work within you, energizing you from within!"***

"So now your obedience is no longer limited to a guilt effort, to obligation and duty, to a guilt

trip, to 'I owe you something' or 'I owe it to you', or 'oh brother, you know, I have been such a bad person, and I am really going to become a good person now: I'm just going to start to pray harder, and I am going to give it all I've got. I'm going to start studying harder, and fast more often, and longer, and go to church as often as I possibly can.'"

...But after a while, you see, *I become disappointed at my own efforts again.*

But hey no, it doesn't work that way my friend; *that way doesn't work!*

But now hey listen; *the Word, the truth of the gospel, does all the work within me; it releases a fire in my heart. It releases and inspires my spirit with God's own initiative, with God's own energy!*

And so you see, *it inevitably spills over into my life; in everything I am and everything I do!*

When God created seed, whether it's pumpkin or peach, He designed that seed with enough energy imprinted into that little computer memory bank, into that computerized programmed little vehicle of a seed, **to release life after its own kind!**

You will never find a pumpkin seed having to borrow life from another kind of seed.

57

There is enough life which God destined for that seed *hidden within it* to produce a full harvest, a mature harvest.

And in the same way, God has built into His vehicle; He has built into His voice, into His Word, into His gospel, *enough truth, enough faith energy, enough love;* **every measure of spirit energy and ability; of wisdom, and knowledge, and truth and understanding; every measure of love and life,** *which you and I could ever need in this life to enable us to walk worthy* of the One who called us by His grace *to His own excellence and glory.*

Chapter 5

No Longer Outsiders, But Family

You see, if the enemy could snare us into one thing, he would do this very thing: he would seek to bring **a distance between the effect of the Word in our hearts, and our own efforts,** so that we can again become conscious of some lack in our lives, *and begin to employ our own efforts again.* This is the essence of hypocrisy when measured by God's standard, *because it's an attempt to **add** something to what we again think and believe we lack in our own lives.*

We are still on the subject of **properly, accurately, appropriating the truth of the gospel.** I want us to take a thorough look at this *in its full implication and weight,* as far as our private devotional life is concerned. I am talking about *our personal embrace of the truth of the gospel **within our hearts,** because it directly affects our lives.*

In our appropriation of the truth of the gospel, we need to really discover to its full extent, to its full conclusion, **the full implication of these things; the full implications of the gospel,** as it relates to our fellowship, and as it relates to our evangelism methods and strategies.

*We need to grasp that we are announcing to the world that their trespasses have been totally forgiven! We are announcing to the world that God does not count their trespasses against them! That is exactly what we are announcing to the world, because **that is the truth** of the gospel; that is **the accurate content** of the gospel!*

His appeal to them through us now is <u>His love</u> and nothing else!

Because, He has reconciled them in Christ! He canceled the bond which stood against them with its legal demands!

That is the gospel!

He has destroyed the poison of death, called Sin, in His own body there on that cross! **He has destroyed their guilt! He has blotted out that handwriting against them in the blood of Christ on that cross!**

That is what the truth of the gospel is all about!

And now it is only their hearing with faith; their full embrace of these things, of the love of God, <u>as reality</u>, that qualifies them to fully enter into His provision.

Their comprehension, their grasping of these <u>realities</u>, their believing of it; their believing in the love God has for them, releases them, to embrace Him!

Hallelujah!

Ephesians 3:14-15 says (And I am reading to you from the Ruach Translation),

"The awesomeness of these redemption realities compels me into urgent prayer as I bow my knees before the Father on your behalf. ***His legitimate Fatherhood legally extends His name to every family both in the heavenlies and here upon the earth.****"*

Some people are so confused about what grace represents that they accuse us of saying that we no longer preach or need Jesus to be a mediator. They even go as far as accusing us of saying that we no longer need to pray in the name of Jesus! *But none of those false assumptions and accusations is true. That is not what we teach.*

We know full well that no man comes to the Father, *but through Him!*

And the fact that He has given us His name means infinitely more than just religiously using His name at the end of our prayers.

What I mean is that I, as a son, wouldn't come to my dad and say to him, "*Dad can I just quickly speak to you in the name of Louw please?"*

Ha... ha... ha...

No. Listen, He takes it for granted that I carry his name. By birth his name was extended to me.

Glory! Thank you Father!

But you see we have become so religious in our respective understanding of what the name of Jesus means.

Listen man, it's not wrong to pray in His name. It's not even wrong to end your prayers with, IN THE NAME OF JESUS. I still daily pray in His name! So don't get legalistic and dogmatic, *even if you now think you have a more enlightened understanding than me.* Don't look at someone in a strange way and think, *'Man, you don't know what I know; you don't know THIS revelation yet. If only you knew OUR revelation: we don't pray ignorantly like that, like you, anymore.'*

Hey listen, I understand grace and teach it fully *and I still pray like that!* It is good to keep praying in the name of Jesus!

But I want everyone to enlarge their understanding of what it means *to be included in the name of Jesus.*

It means that everything that the household of Deity has to offer the human race *is extended to you on legal, valid terms!*

You are no longer an outsider, a sojourner, or a foreigner! *You are a family member of God; a valid member of His household!*

And do you know how strongly God confirms what I just said? **His very own Holy Spirit cries out within your own spirit, "ABBA – *Father, meaning; Daddy God!"***

Not, *"ABBA – Father, in the Name of Jesus…"* no, just *"ABBA,"* or *"Father,"* or *"Daddy,"* **because the Father Himself is your true daddy: your papa,** *and He loves you immensely!*

Listen, in the incarnation, in Christ, the Father Himself *made a personal appearance!*

"God was personally present in Christ when He reconciled the world to Himself!"

"God so very much loved the world that He gave…"

"God demonstrated His own love towards us in this: that even while we were yet sinners, Christ came and He died for us!"

Hey, don't worry: Jesus is not nervous when you become intimate with the Father! **He and the Father are one!**

63

Jesus doesn't feel jealous over your relationship with the Father! **He died for that very thing!**

He gave His very life so you and the Father can have that relationship restored between you!

So don't get religious on us grace preachers, alright? Hang in there and just listen, okay? Just keep reading and open your heart and your mind so that you don't *miss out!*

God is introducing and restoring powerful revelation to the Church today, so don't shut us down, okay? **Don't rob yourself of the increase and depth of intimacy God wants to bring into your life!**

Open your heart and mind!

Don't get distracted if what we say contradicts what you have heard and sounds wrong when you first hear it.

Just stay open and ask God to show you if what we are saying lines up with the truth of the Gospel written about in the Scriptures; *not your favorite doctrine,* amen. Ask Him and He will show you.

Hey man, listen, ha... ha... ha... your Bible is right. You're right. I'm right. This new Mirror Study Bible is also right: we're all right, okay? As long as we love God we're alright! So, tell yourself **we're alright, it's going to be just fine!**

Ha... ha... ha...

It reminds me of a joke I heard once.

A philosopher, I don't remember exactly who it was supposed to be, but this guy said something like this,

"You know, the whole world's wrong. Only ye and me are right ...and even ye are a little bit queer!"

Ha… ha… ha…

If I was to start sharing details with you, you would be amazed of what we have been accused of preaching! We have been accused of preaching the greatest heresies and many other things. We have been shot down and disregarded and ignored, and you name it, if you can imagine it, whatever it may be, no matter how strange or ridiculous, we have probably been accused of it.

But in the realm of eternal reality, and in the light of the truth of the gospel clearly revealed in Paul's writings and the rest of the apostle's writings, *in the light of that gospel,* we are right.

And those who falsely accuse us, just because they haven't heard these things before, and just because out of fear they prefer to cling to their old wrong doctrine and teachings, *have no clue what they are talking about!*

I wonder when men and women of God, supposed leaders in the body of Christ, are going to wake up, grow up, *and start listening to the witness of their own hearts,* **instead of allowing themselves to get caught up in the latest gossip and in the ignorance and mob mentality of their friends and peers?**

I apologize if it sounds like I am on a tirade and coming across too strong, as if trying to defend myself. I really am not. *My concern is that many have closed their ears **and are getting robbed from understanding the gospel more fully.***

I want to make the point again: **The whole reason for Jesus' death was to restore an intimacy and quality of relationship and fellowship with God the Father which the sin and fall of Adam robbed Man of.**

Listen, Jesus has restored to you and me the very same freedom that He Himself enjoys with His Father!

He has restored to us the very same access, the very same blamelessness.

And that is why we worship Him as our one and only mediator!

We worship Him as the One who loved us enough to take our place, and who in our

place was condemned by men and despised and rejected. We worship Him as the way, as the life, as the truth! We worship Him as the clearest unveiling of truth, the clearest unveiling of who God really is, the God who is love, the clearest unveiling of the Father, the Son and the Spirit.

We also worship Him as the clearest unveiling of who we are; *our true identity!*

He came to make Love Himself known in His fullness, *and He also revealed our origin in Him; our sonship.*

Our authentic original design was on display there in Him! Thus, He came to unveil and restore our true identity and we worship Him for it!

He was and is the exact representation, the very image and likeness of the invisible God on display: the very God who is love, and *in whose image and likeness we are all made!*

And therefore we proclaim boldly that no one comes to the Father, *to an accurate intimate revelation of, and relationship with, the Father,* but through Him!

Hallelujah!

And we also therefore proclaim boldly that *no one comes to an accurate intimate revelation of, and relationship with, themselves; with their true identity; their true selves, but through Him!*

He is the very Source and Blueprint of our very being; *we can only discover and define ourselves accurately in Him!*

"In Christ all the fullness of the Godhead dwells, in bodily form, and your completeness is also on display, there, in Him!" - Colossians 2:9-10.

So please don't fall into the same trap as Israel, as the Jews, as the religious world in the days when the Word became flesh and dwelt among them. They had become so familiar, or so they thought, with the prophetic word and with the Scriptures, *that they **never really understood or drew any real benefit from the revelation of the incarnation.*** Just like their ancestors, a people of promise, who died in the wilderness: a people who had a legal and powerful covenant with God, but they died outside of that covenant, **outside of obtaining what that covenant made available to them.** They were so familiar **with their religious doctrine, with the promise, with their prophetic doctrine of the promise,** that they died in the wilderness, **outside of possessing that Land of Promise.** Let us not also get stuck in the same way, *living in some prophetic future mode,* **and missing out on entering in and enjoying reality now, as God has revealed it, and given it to us, in Jesus!**

Chapter 6

Ceasing Our Labors to Enter Rest!

Ephesians 3:15 says,

"His Fatherhood legally extends His name to every family, both in the heavenlies and here upon the earth"

Verse 16,

"My request to the Father…"

Paul writes this epistle and prays this prayer from the urgency of his spirit, urgently appealing to this church, to this group of people, and really to the Church at large, and to the whole Gentile world, *to discover the wealth of their redemption.*

And so he says in verse 16,

"My request to the Father is this: that He may give you, according to the rich measure of His opinion of you (...according to the rich measure of His glory, of His DOXA, of His **favorable opinion of you** *– the word 'glory' in this context literally means, 'opinion'.)*

Thus Paul says,

*"My request to the Father is this: that He may give you, **according to the rich measure of His opinion of you** to be strengthened in the inner-man, **and become mighty,** or **spiritually strong**, through the power of His Spirit at work there, within the inner-man."*

Now verse 17 basically says that,

*"(God's Spirit is working there, in your inner-man, **through the truth, through the rich measure of God's opinion of you;** of who you are, as His child), so that you will become rooted and firmly established **in the love-plan of God, <u>drawing your nourishment from His love revelation</u>** and finding your strength and your stability in that."*

*"Faith brings **a consciousness** of Christ's residence in your heart."*

What is the hope of glory? What produces that glory?

His rich indwelling!

Colossians 2:6 says,

*"As we have received Christ Jesus through our hearing with faith, so we now walk **conscious of our union with Him!"***

It is that very consciousness *that supplies us with the working of God in our inner-man. It supplies us with that energy which He mightily inspires within us!*

70

It is absolutely vital for us to discover the principle of entering into **His** rest, where we cease from our own labors.

How do I strive to enter into his rest, Rudi?

How do I reconcile these two concepts of striving and resting, without contradicting myself in my own theology?

This has truly confused so many sincere believers because one Sunday the preacher is a faith preacher and the next he is a works preacher.

The one Sunday everyone is encouraged, because, o hallelujah, it is a faith appropriation.

But the next Sunday, oh woe is me, brother, because now it is: *"You better be diligent in your conduct!"*

*…And so, unfortunately, absolutely frustrated individuals are **the only real results** of that kind of ministry!*

But I thank God that He doesn't get frustrated with us.

His level of persistence and faithfulness exceeds His disappointment with us sometimes.

He will prevail against our blindness and ignorance and hardness of heart. *He is stubborn in His love!*

Ha... ha... ha... Hallelujah!

He who began a good work, will perfect that work! He will perfect it on the same basis; *on the basis of His own initiative.*

He will perfect it upon no other premise, no other basis, and no other law than **the law of His own faith:** *the law of His own initiative, impacting us!*

Praise God, **He is not going to give up on His design of you, and for you!**

He designed you for His Word, for the truth of that Word to be mightily at work within you, *bringing you to a perfect expression of all that is already within you, awakened by that very Word, and that very Spirit of God, at work within you!*

Another translation of Ephesians 3:17 reads,

"This is the urgency of my desire: that your capacity to accommodate the indwelling Christ will be greatly enlarged, through the working of His power in your inner-man. ***The wealth of His glory (or His opinion) measures that power; it measures the capacity, the largeness of His ability at work within you!"***

What is **the full measure of God's ability** at work within me? It's according to my faith, amen; *my discovery and insight and revelation into the truth of the Gospel.*

What is the full measure of God's working within me?

Is it the goose bumps I get?

Hallelujah for the goose bumps. I love the goose bumps, *but I don't build my faith on goose bumps!*

I will not allow my faith to be altered or affected *based upon whether I have the goose bumps or not!*

What is the full measure of His favor?

I mean **how do I measure that?**

By conduct? Or by faith; by His faith in me, His love for me, revealed in Jesus?

What's the full measure of His attitude towards me?

I mean, **what guarantees God's consistency,** His consistent involvement in my life?

What **guarantees** God's **blessings?**

My conduct? Or simply my faith; my appreciation which awakens my trust in Him?

What guarantee do I have that God is not going to give up on me tomorrow …*That maybe tomorrow God is also going to have just another manic Monday and wake up in a bad mood and just suddenly decide, "Listen I've* *had enough. Enough is enough! Angels, that's it; I've had it: I'm just going to cut this guy off. I never want any of you mentioning his name before Me ever again!*

What's the guarantee that that won't happen?

What's my **guarantee?**

The measure of the wealth of His eternal opinion of me *is my guarantee!*

His tremendous love for me *is my guarantee!*

How do I measure **His opinion?**

How do I measure *the wealth of it?*

How do I measure the wealth of His dream concerning me; *that dream of which I am the fulfillment of?*

Looking into the face of Jesus! Discovering the love of God for me *there! That's how I measure that wealth!*

Looking into the face of Jesus! *Looking into that blameless innocence! Looking into the eyes of a lover! Looking into the eyes of favor! Seeing in His eyes the heart-dream of God extended to the human race!*

...Seeing the heart of God on display <u>there</u>!

That's how I measure that wealth!

Paul says that I am looking <u>at Him</u> *as in a mirror!*

And while <u>looking at Him</u> *and the wealth of His favorable opinion of me on display,* **I am transformed!**

While <u>looking at Him</u> **I am transformed *into the same likeness!***

Because I discover myself there!

I discover the truth of who I really am in God's opinion <u>*there*</u>!

I discover that I am loved and that I am indeed God's offspring!

I am transformed because I discover my true self <u>*there*</u>; my God designed self!

While <u>looking at Him</u> **I am transformed into the same likeness *from glory to glory!***

The glory of the flesh, my own fleshly opinion of who I am is done away with, and what I am left with is His glory; His original glory within me! That glory is restored to me in full!

And so, His glory becomes my glory!

His exact expression of the glory; of the opinion of God, of our one and only true Father, *becomes my expression too!*

Hallelujah!

Thank you Jesus!

Jesus is the One **making visible *the invisible!***

His majesty becomes my mirror!

His glory becomes my glory!

It is so wonderful to discover that I no longer need to stare at the Law: *I no longer have to stare and wonder in confusion at a mirror reflecting the insufficiency of my own effort.*

I am now beholding, I'm gazing, upon a mirror that reflects brightly the glory of God in the face of Christ: *In the face of a man.*

We have <u>this treasure</u> in earthen vessels.

"...according to the wealth of His opinion of you!"

Isn't that just awesome? Hallelujah!

It's that very wealth that releases a working within you, which takes you beyond your own effort!

So we might as well relax **and yield to a new law; the law of faith, the law of righteousness by faith.**

Paul bears witness to the zealous religious efforts of his own nation in Romans 10:1. He says,

*"I bear them witness that they do have a zeal; a fiery inspiration for God, **but it's not enlightened**."*

Listen: it's merely a zeal inspired by a guilt-consciousness, a sense of inadequacy, a sense of lack. And tomorrow I am going to beat and buffet myself more, and I am going to really work at it harder. I'm going to really get there: I'll show the world I'll get there! But they're left with having to admit at the end of the arduous race, at the end of the struggle: *"O wretched man that I am, the very thing the Law educated me to do and to try and be, I found my own heart contradicting."*

Let's read on there in Ephesians Chapter Three.

In the light of this working within you, verse 18 says,

*"…then you will take full possession, together with all the saints of the limitless dimension of His love. You will comprehend the breadth and the length and the height and the depth, and intimately know the love of Christ, **which exceeds every limit of sense-governed knowledge**."*

You see, because there is this knowledge which I obtain through my five senses (smell, touch, taste, hearing and sight – It is my contact with my natural environment, through my five senses), and I live my life by this sense-governed knowledge, *together with everyone else ...having to behave up to this person's standard, and up to that one's opinion.*

But Paul says that this revelation *of **His** approval, and of **His** love,* **gives Him energy to live within me,** *beyond every limit!*

*"**It is within the scope of this unveiling** that the fullness of God will flood your life,"* he goes on to say there in Ephesians.

Verse 20 says,

*"His super-abundant ability to do within us **by His love**, far beyond what we ask Him to do, or even thought that He would do, **is the very power that now energizes us from within**."*

(Do you see how ridiculously restricted we were in our religious concepts of Him?)

*"**The wealth of His opinion of us, and of His very achievement in Christ, becomes the reservoir of strength and energy within us!**"*

Paul says in Verse 21,

*"His glory is now manifested in both **the Church** ...and in Christ Jesus"*

(*"His glory is now manifested in **the Church,** in the EKKLESIA, in the ones called out of this natural mindset, out of that prison, out of that darkness, out of that hell, out of the sense-knowledge ruled mindset of this world,* **by seeing their true identity revealed and restored there in Christ and in the work of redemption!**)

"His glory is now manifested, both in them, the Church, and in Christ Jesus, as an eternal trophy throughout all generations."

Listen, what God is now able to do in us, *through insight into these things,* **what God is now able to manifest within His Church,** *is not in any way inferior to what He was able to manifest and communicate through Christ!*

If we understand this revelation of what is within us to be the very basis of God's working within us, *as the energy that He inspires within us,* we will never again feel the need to go back to our own works. We will never again be snared into our own works mentality again, into employing our own efforts *to add to what God has revealed and achieved and redeemed in Christ!*

Listen, it is so wonderful to discover that **He is indeed the Alpha of His own word and of His own work.**

In the remaining books in this series, I am going to do my best to teach you *the practical application of these things* in the light of this enormous truth.

Chapter 7

Faith is the Key!

Let's just quickly go to Romans nine and ten, and we will close with that.

Paul in Romans 9:30 talks about the fact that the Gentiles, those who had no claim to the promise through natural birth, and who did not pursue righteousness, *have attained it* by faith.

And then he goes on to say that Israel, who pursued righteousness did not succeed in obtaining righteousness under the Law, their own inconsistency keeping them out, because they based righteousness on the law.

He says, *"...but they did not succeed in fulfilling the Law."*

Romans 9:32,

"Why? Because they did not pursue that life the law pointed to, through faith."

What did they not pursue *through faith?*

God's approval, God's recognition, which produces that kind of life the Law merely pointed to.

So, if they did not pursue discovering God's recognition *through faith,* then how then did they pursue God's recognition?

Through their own works and their own conduct.

Paul says,

"…but they did not pursue it through faith, but (they pursued it) as if it were based on works (instead of faith)."

He says,

"They have stumbled over the stumbling stone,"

"…just as it is written, Behold, I am laying in Zion a stone that will make men stumble; a rock that will make them fall;"

*"…and yet **he who believes in Him** will not be put to shame."*

Why will it offend Man; why would what God did in Jesus offend Man?

Because Man rejected Him!

I mean, you know, that's not really our kind of a stone, not the kind foundation we expected and wanted.

"Lord, who will believe our report," says Isaiah in Isaiah 53:1.

I mean He looks and seems so insignificant in His appearance, He's not the type of macho man we had in mind!

...And then He dies on a cross and He becomes a curse: *what a failure, what a disappointment to our expectation!*

We could have crowned Him as our new king just on the basis of His supernatural powers and His works of miracles, *but then He goes and dies on us, hanging there on that cross so weak and so helpless!*

Thus, He became *"...a stumbling stone that will make men stumble; a rock that will make men fall..."*

What is that rock?

Righteousness **by faith!**

That's Jesus; *righteousness **by faith.*** That's Jesus; *that's what He's all about!*

And the Scriptures says,

*"...and **he who believes in Him** will not be put to shame."*

"As many as received Him..." - John 1:12

*"He came **to His own**..."* - Verse 11

...**but His own rejected Him!**

83

"...but as many as received Him..."

How do I receive Him?

Through faith, through embracing the truth revealed in Jesus, through embracing the work of redemption, through embracing that truth, as reality, through embracing Him!

I receive Him through simply seeing and agreeing and embracing what is revealed and accomplished there in Him, in the whole incarnation, and work of redemption!

"...he who believes in Him will not be ashamed..."

We will not be <u>ashamed</u>.

Then Romans 10:1 says,

"Brethren, my heart's desire and prayer to God for them (that's for the Jews, the religious folk; the legalistic, Law-of-works-bound religious folk) *is that they may be saved* (rescued).*"*

How are they rescued?

Through hearing with faith!

*"I bear them witness that they have a zeal for God, **but it is not enlightened.**"*

Verse 3,

"For being ignorant of the righteousness that comes from God, and seeking to establish their own, they did not yield (or submit) *to God's righteousness."*

Now in appropriating what God has made available to us in this covenant, *we need to understand what it means* **to yield** *to God's righteousness.*

Verse 17 of Romans 10 says,

*"...**faith <u>comes</u>** by hearing..."*

Hearing what?

Hearing the Word; hearing the gospel.

Faith <u>comes</u> by listening to the truth of the gospel <u>*and embracing it*</u>.

Faith comes by hearing and <u>agreeing</u> with the LOGOS revealed in Jesus; *hearing that <u>revelation</u> of Christ – what He came to reveal!*

You see, faith **comes,** it literally **COMES** to you; *it is **imparted to you**, through the hearing of the gospel,* and you literally have to resist that faith that comes to you, and reject it for some or the other reason, **in order for you not to be affected by it,** ha... ha... ha... Hallelujah!

But you see, if you do not resist, if you do not reject it, but instead *yield to it,* I mean, **as you embrace it, as you receive it, as you agree** with God, *His faith takes root in you and it begins to bear it's fruit in your heart and life!*

Oh, hallelujah!

Romans 10:4 goes on to say,

"For Christ is the end of the Law,"

"...so that every single one who has faith may be justified."

...Every single one!

Through the hearing with faith.

Father, we treasure the working of Your Word within us *as our greatest wealth!*

And so, Father, we would say to You that, *abiding in Your Word* is greater to us than even a number one priority!

It has truly become to us **our only priority** in life: **a genuine addiction, a perfectly good addiction; an ecstasy!**

…We are continuing in Your Word, *through faith,* and thus we are now also continuing in faith, *through Your Word* …through the washing of that water of your Word!

…Thus, continuing in Your Word *and having Your Word continue in us,* **is our only priority *and an ecstasy to us!***

We thank you for the knowledge of the truth which brings **liberty!**

…And I thank you, Father, that through my books, and through the Scriptures expounded on in these books, *and through the hearing of faith,* men and women are released and set free from every evidence of darkness in their life!

Thank you that You have indeed extended to every individual reading these books, *to those who have an ear to hear,* You have extended Your Word, the very LOGOS; Christ Himself – *the Christ-life!*

Thank you, Father, that You have extended in Your Word, and thus in these words, **the absoluteness of Your favor, and You have extended Your total unequivocal forgiveness, and the totality of Your redemption and reconciliation** *…so that we may respond through faith and embrace Your Word with joy!*

Hallelujah!

Thank you Jesus!

We thank you that when the light **comes to us, when the light is introduced, through the gospel,** *darkness goes!*

If you are reading this, and you are conscious of any lack in your life, of any lack in your health, of any lack in your spirit-fellowship with

God, any blockage in your own mental understanding of the Word, any lack that would possibly intimidate the design of the Creator in your life, *I want you to simply expose your heart and life to the sunlight of His Word; simply* **embrace His love!**

Embrace the truth of the gospel, and embrace His love for you, and allow Him to dispel that darkness!

Let your spirit-man come alive **fully!**

Let faith come alive *fully* within you!

Let Him inspire a new energy within you!

That energy of faith.

If you let it have its perfect work, it will release the very faith of God within you! *It will release the very ability of God within you!*

Beholding Him in His fullness, face to face in His full beauty; the beauty of who He is and the purity of His love for you, *you are transformed!*

So, as you have heard these things and are hearing these things, **embrace the Word fully,** it is my plea to you! Embrace it in your bosom, for it is truly worthy of all acceptance! I say again: **Embrace it fully and let Jesus Christ become the revelation *which your heart has always yearned for,* amen.**

You know, **our communion; our intimate fellowship within the Godhead in our union with Christ Jesus** *and our full embrace of what He both revealed and accomplished* **and opened up for us to enter into and enjoy, is so sacred, so holy; It's at the core of our very ongoing encounter with God our Father, our Daddy, our Papa, and Jesus, our precious Lord, in the dimension and environment of the Holy Spirit of Truth!**

Therefore, we cannot afford to get distracted from the depth of the truth; from the depth of what it really communicates, and lose out **on the richness of that oneness** *God Himself has called us into when He invited us into the very fellowship of the Son;* **that very intimate fellowship the Son Himself enjoys within the Godhead!** - 1 Corinthians 1:9.

In closing, let's take a look at one more Scripture, but this time our of the Mirror Study Bible, because it brings out so clearly what I want to emphasize and leave you with in this book. Let's go to 1 Corinthians 11:23-34 and end in 1 Corinthians 12:3.

11:23 Let me remind you then (says Paul) what we are actually celebrating in our fellowship meal:

The very night in which the Lord Jesus was betrayed, He took BREAD

11:24 and gave thanks; breaking the BREAD into portions, he said, "1Realize

**your complete association with my death
and resurrection, every time you eat,
remember my body that was broken for
you!"**

*(Meaning 1take, or **grasp** [LAMBAMO is the
Greek word], actually saying **to take what is
one's own**, or **to fully associate something
with or unto one's self**.)*

**11:25 He did exactly the same thing with
the cup after partaking of the supper and
said, "This cup holds and represents the
mystery of the wine of the New Covenant
fully reestablished in my blood; therefore
you celebrate me afresh and anew, every
time you drink, with this solid and proper
understanding!"**

*(From now on our regular every day meals,
whether alone or with one another, are all very
meaningful. We all celebrate the fact that **the
incarnation reveals both our redemption
and our oneness;** because the promise
became a person and was then fulfilled.*

*This person, Jesus Christ, redeemed our
original value, identity, innocence and
oneness; he died our death and defines the life
of oneness with Deity and with one another we
now live. He completely fulfills the entire
theme of Scripture, which is: the sufferings of
the Messiah **and the subsequent glory!** [1
Peter 1:10-11])*

11:26 Your every meal therefore makes the
1mandate of his 2coming absolutely
relevant again to you, and communicates to
your inner-being, and to others, the full
meaning of the New Covenant.

*(Whether you eat or drink, you are declaring
your joint inclusion in his death, resurrection
and ascension, **confirming your redeemed
innocence, and therefore your oneness
with Deity restored**. Some translations read,
"until I come..." as if he never came and now
his coming is again put off until some future
date.*

*Listen, the word translated as **until**, is 1ACHRI,
which come from AKMEN, which means,
extremity, conclusion. It refers to **the
present time;** thus it speaks of **the extremity
of a conclusion reached in the present time,**
or **which absolutely ultimately affects the
present time – it alters our present reality.***

*Jesus is the absolute ultimate conclusion of
prophetic time!*

*The word, 2ERCHOMAI, incorrectly translated
in most of our translations as **to come**, is
actually written in the original language in the
Aorist Subjective Mood, ELTHE, which is
similar to the OPTATIVE expressing of a wish.
The Mood of the Greek verb expresses the
mode in which the idea of the verb is
employed. Thus, what Paul is saying is that
we are communicating the desire to have*

91

all people realize the FULL meaning of the New Covenant.

*In relation to this, see 2 Peter 1:19, "For us the appearing of the Messiah **is no longer a future promise** to have to try and hold on to, but **a fulfilled reality. Now it is your turn to have more than a second-hand, hear-say experience and testimony. Now it is your turn to have your own REAL experience and testimony, that fully matches ours.** So, take my word as one would take a lamp at night; now picture this: The day is about to dawn for you **in your own understanding and encounter.** When the Morning Star appears to you in full glory, you no longer need the lamp; **this is exactly what will happen to you shortly, on the horizon of your own hearts and within your own spirits.**")*

11:27 So, whoever does not truly value the full meaning of the true BREAD and of the genuine (New Testament) WINE, keep themselves in condemnation (unnecessarily so).

11:28 To see oneself completely and fully associated in Christ's death and then declared totally innocent in his blood, and therefore utterly embraced again in oneness with the Godhead, is the only worthy manner in which to examine one's own life, in the context of the New Covenant, New Testament meal we celebrate.

*(Self examination according to the Old Covenant, i.e. Deuteronomy 28 **is no longer relevant.** "Examine yourselves to see for yourselves whether you are holding to the real faith; discover yourselves there in the Faith of God; come on, test and examine that faith for yourselves, do you not also then realize that Jesus Christ in all his fullness is within you!?" [2 Corinthians 13:5 – Read the RSV Translation also.)*

11:29 Anyone who partakes of this meal of communion; this meal celebrating our oneness with Deity, in an indifferent manner, either because of nonsensical religious sentiment, or merely being blasé about the depth of the real meaning of the meal, still eats and drinks their own condemnation and judgments they hold onto within themselves! Hey, the human body of Jesus represents the judgment and acquittal of every single human life; to fail to now acknowledge this reality is to deliberately exclude yourself from the enormous immediate blessing of the New Testament and its New Covenant relationship of oneness with the Godhead.

(Isaiah 53:3-8, "He was despised and rejected by men; a man who partook of all our sorrows, and became most intimately acquainted with our many griefs, but still, we esteemed him not. Hey, surely he has borne away our pains, and carried off our disease; yet, we didn't recognize him for what he did, but instead, in unbelief,

*and in our misconceptions about God and we He really is, we esteemed him (the Messiah) rather as one who was stricken, and smitten by God, and severely afflicted by Him, in our illusions and deception. But, he was wounded **by** our transgressions, he was bruised **by** our iniquities; yes, upon him fell the chastisement we handed out, and which in the end made us whole. Oh yes, with his stripes we are healed – made completely whole! All we, like sheep, have gone astray; we have all turned to his or her own way; yes, every single one of us did; but the Lord has laid the burden of us all, that burden of our iniquities, on him, on his heart, to bear and carry it off and away. Like a lamb that is led to the slaughter, and like a sheep that before its shearers is dumb, so he opened not his mouth. By oppression and judgment he was taken away; and as for his generation, who even considered that he was cut off out of the land of the living, stricken **by** the very transgression of my people?" [Read the RSV also.]* **No one can afford to underestimate what happened to us all on the cross, and in the resurrection, and in the ascension** *also. [Ephesians 2:4-7].* **To discern the Lord's body correctly, accurately, is to fully grasp what God's faith saw when Jesus died and cried, "It is finished!"***)*

11:30 This is the very reason why many of you are suffering unnecessarily with weaknesses and <u>illnesses</u> and many have already fallen asleep (spiritually), and many

of them have then also even physically died <u>prematurely</u>.

11:31 By correctly judging that we indeed co-died in his death, and were indeed also co-raised to newness of life in his resurrection, we walk in freedom from any kind of judgment!

(John 5:22, "The Father judges no one, but has given all judgment to the Son." [RSV] John 12:31-33, "Now is the judgment of this world, now shall the ruler of this world be cast out; and I, when I am lifted up from the earth, will draw all judgment to myself." He said this to show by what death he was about to die.")

11:32 By discerning the broken body of Christ correctly, accurately, we can only ultimately conclude that he suffered our brokenness and distortion; *this is the full teaching of the gospel,* **and the ultimate instruction of the Lord: What foolishness it would now indeed be to still continue to place yourself and the rest of the world under judgment,** *when Jesus already took all judgment upon himself!***?**

11:33 So, when you come together to eat a meal together and celebrate the Covenant communion and oneness we enjoy with the Lord, embrace one another in love's full embrace with utmost courtesy; holding no judgments against each other.

11:34 There is no point in getting together while you are still competing and comparing yourselves among yourselves, judging one another and one upping one another, seeing who can be the most spiritual by eating or drinking the most! Hey, eat at home first if you are that hungry; why turn a celebration of oneness and of Him into condemnation; into yet another guilt and inferiority trip!?

*(Our love-feasts [our **ordinary every-day meals** which is transformed into something sacred we share between us and the Lord; that sacred **faith** of God] now celebrates the success of the cross and resurrection and ascension, and has nothing in common with any pagan banquet or sex-orgy!*

*The prophetic picture of the table was most sacred and significant! The priests had to **daily** place **fresh BREAD** on the table in the sanctuary – just like we do with our constant meditation in our inner-man upon the heavenly realities, or spirit-realities, revealed in Jesus; I am talking about that life the Word affords us in our inner-man; that abundant life, that BREAD of life, that eternal life, that bliss we enjoy in our abiding within the full embrace; within the very bosom of our Father.*

The BREAD the priests had to daily place of the table in the sanctuary was called, SHOWBREAD, or in Hebrew, LECHEM

*HAPANIM, literally meaning: "**Face-bread** or; **Bread of the Presence**". Wow!*

*The Hebrew word for **presence** means, **face to face!***

While Jesus spoke to the two disciples on their way to Emmaus in Luke 24, they did not recognize him, even though their hearts ignited while he was pointing to himself in Scripture, explaining the prophetic promise of mankind's full redemption, beginning with Moses and his writings, and going through the Psalms, and all the Prophets, he highlighted what was said, but gave it context as he was explaining to them how it all fit together and culminated in the person, death and resurrection of the Messiah. In Luke's interview, he pressed them for every detail of their conversation with the resurrected Jesus on that road to Emmaus; he wanted to know exactly at what point in their meeting with Jesus did they recognize him in his person! He writes in verse 28, "So, they drew near to the village to which they were going, and Jesus appeared to be going further..."

Wow! Should Jesus not at this point at least given them an opportunity to make a commitment, or at least say a "sinners prayer" or something similar to it?

But hey no; not even the best Rabbi could take them any further! The full embrace of what was being said, and actually enter into that communion around the truth, entering into fellowship and oneness with Him, was up to them!

*Luke 24:29, "**But they themselves constrained him,** saying, "Sir, stay with us, for it is toward evening and the day is now far spent." **So he went in to stay with them."***

*Luke 24:30, "**When he was at the table with them, he took the bread and blessed, and broke it, and gave it to them."***

*Luke 24:31, "**And suddenly then their eyes were opened and they recognized him;** and then he vanished from their sight."*

Instead of disappointment, a great excitement now arrested their hearts, and so, they took off in the middle of the night even, desiring to tell the others back in Jerusalem all that they have experienced, and are experiencing.

Listen; nothing mobilizes one more than realizing the absolute relevance of the revelation of the incarnation!

*You see, they knew that Jesus could no longer be any more present in his person, than what he is, **present** right now, right there **in the Word ...alive in us**; in the Word **fully digested ...fully incarnate within us!***

*The moment we discover Jesus in Scripture **as in a mirror,** it is then that our hearts finally ignite and our very next meal becomes a*

*celebration of the incarnation and of our
oneness with Deity restored!*

*"Every time you eat and drink be conscious of
me! Remember fondly but soberly what I
accomplished and made available for you to
enjoy!" – Jesus.*

*Our every meal now celebrates the temple –
the lives we enjoy right now and right here
even in these flesh and blood bodies.*

*Our every meal celebrates the temple – the
reality that we now are the temple of the living
God, His very inner sanctuary, the holy of
holies, where God abides, in Spirit form, in all
His fullness!*

*"He who is joined to the Lord is one Spirit with
Him! " Spirit to spirit combined; oneness
celebrated!*

*Hey, how wonderful, how marvelous, your
body is God's address on planet earth!*

*He does not dwell in buildings made by human
hands.*

*Wow! You will never again need to employ
your willpower to diet and get into shape,
spiritually or naturally! Willpower is the inferior
language of the Law! Love and value and
spirit-consciousness has now replaced
willpower! Love and value-consciousness
ignites belief! The **REVELATION** of; the full in-
depth **grasping** of the truth accurately, sets*

you free in your inner-man, to be free indeed! The days of fast-food and junk-food [spiritually speaking] are over! Hey even the days of existing on a constant self-destruct natural diet of fast-food and junk-food are also over! The Table of redemption-realities, and many happy years of fruitful labor, set before us, is sacred to us now, for it fully celebrates these bodies we live in as the very sanctuary of our redeemed lives; that life of our authentic design and our oneness with Deity! Sitting around this Table, The Table of redemption-realities can only mean one thing: A feast of ongoing friendship and deep meaningful delightful conversation! Come on, eat food that blesses the temple, both spiritually and naturally speaking! Do you not know that most diseases are diet-related? And that included the diet your spirit and soul partakes of! Hey, study and stick to nutrition!

...Because, "We have this treasure in earthen vessels!"

...And the vessel most certainly takes its value from the treasure it holds!)

12:1 Spiritual manifestations are supernatural indeed, yet often very practical and natural. Just because God is peaking to you and moving in the spirit dimension, does not mean that you cannot understand what God's Spirit within you is saying to you or wanting to do through you.

12:2 Remember how, when some of you were still practicing pagan worship which you though were so spiritual; do you remember still how you got carried away by dead and dumb idols, ideas, and concepts, into doing many weird and even spooky things.

(Back then you were snared by voiceless idols, and dumb ideas; inferior thoughts and concepts, but now instead, you are indeed empowered by the very voice of God Himself speaking within you. He finds a voice in ordinary people, just like me and you, for we are able and fully equipped to echo and amplify what He is saying to mankind in Christ.)

12:3 Holy Spirit will never distract from Jesus, or prompt anyone ever to dishonor Christ; Holy Spirit will always only magnify Jesus!

*(In Hebrew the word, RUACH or **Spirit,** is neuter general, meaning, **neither male nor female,** but is used in the feminine form, when connected to **the truth** and representing **the truth,** from the Godhead's perspective; **ultimate truth and reality**. This is done deliberately because the Godhead **is expressing their strong desire to impact you** with the truth, from their perspective, ultimate truth, **on a much deeper, emotional, and spiritual level,** and not just on a shallow intellectual level, in which there is still room for*

some kind of distance or disconnect. Thus when the Holy Spirit in detail expresses the truth in depth, it is to take us beyond all distance and disconnect, and to establish oneness God – it is to bring about a marriage and romance between us and God, within the Word; within the context of ultimate truth and love revealed, and intimately understood!

See John 16:13, "But when she, the Spirit of Truth, is come, she will take you gently by the hand and guide you right into the path of all truth, in which a discovery of the reality of what truth unveils, and an inevitable encounter with the ultimate truth, as a person, is unavoidable! She will not feel the need to draw attention to herself, but would much rather communicate and unveil to you everything she hears and thoroughly understands and accurately discerns about things, from a heavenly perspective, especially about things that is able to and will happen to you and through you, from within you!"

*John 16:14, "Holy Spirit will strongly endorse and persuade you of my indwelling glory within you, and of my sure and steadfast opinion of you – your very innocence, as well as your immense value to me, and your true worth! Holy Spirit will take that which is mine, which belongs to me exclusively and makes me who I am, i.e. the truth about me, and she will accurately and thoroughly interpret and explain it to you **as being within you!**)*

Wow, isn't hat just such good news!

It is amen!

...And it's all revealed to be within us!

The entire Bible is about Jesus, the Messiah, and He in turn is not just about revealing the Father to us, *but He also reveals us to us!* **He is the ultimate reality of who God is, and who we are, in our union and oneness with Him, *on open display!***

I urge you to get yourself a copy of the Mirror Study Bible. It is the best translation of the Scriptures from the original Greek that I have ever read, and it's available online at: Barnes & Noble and several other book sellers.

If you want me or someone from of our team to come to where you are, *anywhere in the world,* and give a talk or teach you and some of your friends *about the gospel message and these redemption realities,* simply contact us on www.LivingWordIntl.com ...or you can always find me on Facebook.

If your life has changed as a result of reading this book, *please write to me and let me know.*

I would love to share in your joy *so that my joy in writing this book may be full!*

"That which was from the beginning,

which we have heard
(**with our spiritual ears**),

which we have seen
(**with our spiritual eyes**),

which we have looked upon
(**beheld, focused our attention upon**),

and which our hands have also handled (**which we have also experienced**),

concerning the Word of life,
we declare to you,

that you also
may have this fellowship with us;

and truly
our fellowship is
with the Father
and with His Son
Jesus Christ.

And these things we write to you
that your joy may be full."

— 1 John 1:1-4

About the Author

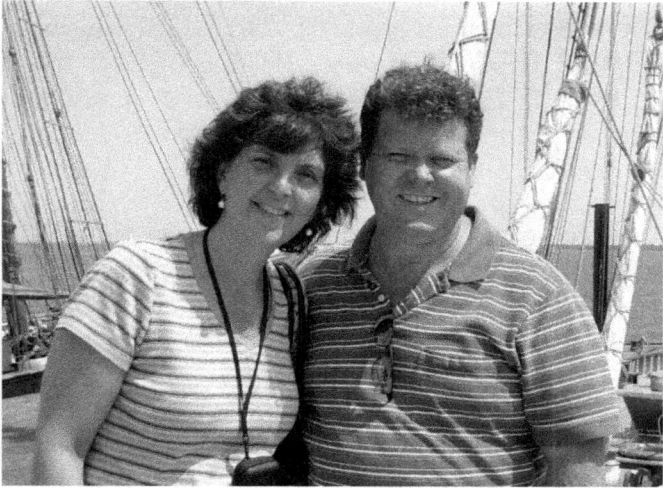

Rudi & Carmen Louw together oversee: Living Word International.

They also travel and minister both locally and internationally.

Rudi was born and raised in the country of South Africa, while Carmen grew up in Cortland, New York.

They function in the ministry of reconciliation (2 Corinthians 5:18-21) and flow strongly with the Holy Spirit and His anointing to teach, preach, prophesy, heal, and whatever is needed to touch people's lives with the reality of God's love and power.

God has given them keen insight into what He has to say to mankind in the work of redemption concerning the revelation and restoration of humanity's true identity.

Therefore they emphasize THE GOSPEL, IN CHRIST REALITIES, the GRACE of God, the WORD OF RIGHTEOUSNESS, *and all such eternal truths essential to salvation and living the CHRIST-LIFE.*

They have been granted this wisdom and revelation into the knowledge of God by the resurrected Spirit of Jesus Christ, *to establish and strengthen believers in the faith of God, and to activate them in ministering to others.*

Not only are people set free from the poison and bondage of sin, condemnation and all kinds of intimidation, (upheld, strengthened and reinforced by age old religious ideas born out of ignorance) **but many are brought into a closer more intimate relationship with Father God, as Daddy**, through accurate teaching and unveiling of the gospel message, prophetic words, healings and miracles.

Rudi & Carmen are closely knitted together with many other effective Christians, church fellowships, and groups of believers who share the same revelation and passion **to impart the truth of the gospel to others, *so as to impact and transform the world we live in with the LOVE and POWER of God.***